TECHNOLOGY OF ANCIENT GREECE

MELANIE ANN APEL

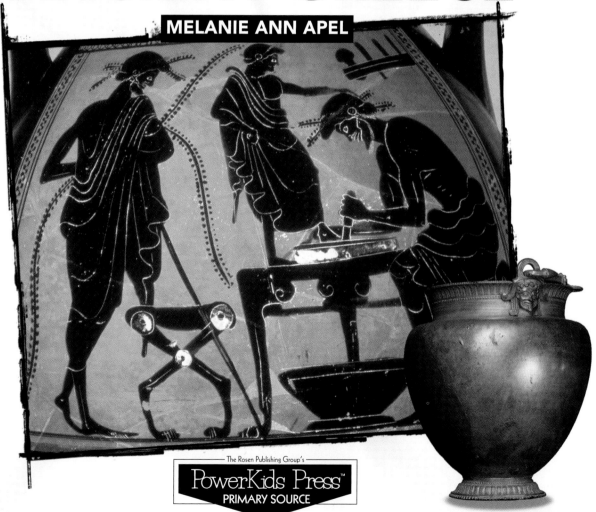

The Rosen Publishing Group's

PowerKids Press™
PRIMARY SOURCE

New York

For Michael. Love, Melanie.

Published in 2004 by The Rosen Publishing Group, Inc.
29 East 21st Street, New York, NY 10010

First Edition

Editor: Joanne Randolph
Book Design: Michael DeGuzman
Layout Design: Kim Sonsky
Photo Researcher: Peter Tomlinson

Photo Credits: Cover (center) Ashmolean Museum, Oxford, U.K./Bridgeman Art Library; cover (right), p. 4 (left) The Art Archive/Archaeological Museum Salonica/Dagli Orti; p. 4 (right) The Art Archive/Museo della Sibaritide Sibari/Dagli Orti; p. 7 © Yann Arthus-Bertrand/CORBIS; p. 7 (inset) British Museum, London, U.K./Bridgeman Art Library; pp. 8, 11 (left and right), 12 The Art Archive/Dagli Orti; p. 11 (center) SEF/Art Resource, NY; p. 15 (top) The Art Archive/Acropolis Museum Athens/Dagli Orti; p. 15 (bottom) Donald A. Frey/Institute of Nautical Archaeology; p. 16 (left) © Archivo Iconigrafico, S.A./CORBIS; p. 16 (center) The Art Archive/National Archaeological Museum Athens/Dagli Orti; p. 16 (right) The Art Archive/Archaeological Museum Nauplia Nafplion/Dagli Orti; p. 19 © Stephanie Colasanti/CORBIS; pp. 19 (inset), 20 (top) Erich Lessing/Art Resource, NY; p. 20 (bottom) Réunion des Musées Nationaux/Art Resource, NY.

Apel, Melanie Ann.
Technology of ancient Greece / Melanie Ann Apel.
    p. cm.—(Primary sources of ancient civilizations. Greece)
Includes bibliographical references and index.
Contents: Technology of Ancient Greece—Agriculture—Indoor plumbing—Architecture—Construction technology—Sailing ships—Weapons—Science and medicine—Tools for surgery—Astronomy and mathematics.
  ISBN 0-8239-6773-5 (library binding)—ISBN 0-8239-8941-0 (paperback)
1. Technology—Greece—History—To 146 B.C.—Juvenile literature. 2. Greece—Civilization—To 146 B.C.—Juvenile literature. [1. Technology—Greece—History. 2. Greece—Civilization—To 146 B.C.] I. Title. II. Series.
  T16.A64 2004
  609.38—dc21

                                                                    2003002792

Manufactured in the United States of America

Contents

Technology of Ancient Greece   5

Agriculture   6

Indoor Plumbing   9

Architecture   10

Construction Technology   13

Sailing Ships   14

Weapons   17

Science and Medicine   18

Tools for Surgery   21

Astronomy and Mathematics   22

Glossary   23

Index   24

Primary Sources   24

Web Sites   24

Greeks created jewelry out of bronze. This bronze set is from the sixth century B.C.

This cauldron, or large pot, was crafted in the fourth century B.C. using bronze. The tripod it stands on is made from iron.

4

Technology of Ancient Greece

Ancient Greek civilization made many advances during its long history. Most of the ancient Greek technology that influences, or affects, modern life was created and used during the Bronze and the Iron Ages. The Bronze Age was a time around 5,000 years ago, when people learned how to make many things, including weapons, from copper and bronze. People shaped these metals by heating them until they became liquid and then pouring them into molds to cool. Around 1000 B.C., the Greeks learned how to craft tools and goods from iron. This called for different technology from that used in shaping copper or bronze. More heat was needed. The heated iron was not a liquid. It had to be shaped by hammering.

Agriculture

In the earliest times, Greek people probably hunted for meat and gathered wild plants for food. As time passed, they began to raise their own animals and to plant seeds for crops. At first farmers used sticks to help them dig. Later, plows were invented. Ancient Greeks also learned how to irrigate crops. Even with these advances, farming was hard in Greece. The soil was rocky, and little rain fell during the year. Men used wooden plows pulled by oxen to cut the soil to be planted. The farmers then had to go back and break up the soil by hand before seeds could be planted. To make the best of poor soil, farmers rotated their crops to maintain the land's fertility. Rotating crops meant that farmers only planted part of their land each season.

Farming in ancient Greece was hard. This modern-day image of Greece shows plots of fertile land between areas of rocky land. ▶

Greek farmers used oxen to pull plows. The plow helped the farmer to dig long ditches in the soil, which could then be planted with seeds.

8

Indoor Plumbing

As early as 432 B.C., many homes in ancient Greece had indoor plumbing. Archaeologists have found the remains of ancient Greek bathtubs that are more than 2,000 years old. Archaeologists think that the Greeks must have used clay pipes to carry water out of the house and into the ground. In addition to bathtubs, ancient Greek homes often had latrines, or toilets. The toilets flushed with water into a sewer system under the street.

Ancient Greeks also kept a supply of drinking water. Pipes or channels called aqueducts carried freshwater from mountain streams to cisterns, or wells. Fountains on the street were connected to the cisterns, and people could draw water when they needed it.

◄ Greek bathrooms, such as this one from the fourteenth century B.C., had toilets and bathtubs. This bath is made of ceramic, a kind of tile.

Architecture

Ancient Greeks built their homes in a simple style. Most houses were made of sun-baked mud bricks. In public buildings, stone came to be used instead of bricks or wood. Greek builders used columns and beams as frames for these buildings. The stone beams were huge in size and rested on many sturdy columns. Columns served as supports for a building's weight, but they were also decorative. The Doric and the Ionic were two basic styles of architecture used on the public buildings of ancient Greece. The Doric column was sturdy and plain. The Ionic column was more decorative. Ionic column tops had scroll-like carvings. Another less popular style in Greece was the fancy Corinthian style, in which columns had carvings of leaves on their tops.

◀ Corinthian columns, such as these, had fancy leaf shapes carved into the top.

Ionic columns, such as this one from Delphi, Greece, had a scroll shape on the ▶ top. The ridges on a column are called flutes.

Doric columns were plain. Notice how ▶ these columns from the Temple of Hera in Olympia, Greece, have simple tops. These columns were built in the seventh century B.C.

Construction Technology

When building large structures, such as temples for their gods, the ancient Greeks used a number of different tools. Slaves went down into a quarry, or a large hole from which stone could be taken. There they cut the rocks used to build the large public buildings. They used wooden, stone, and copper tools to cut the rocks to the size that was needed. A stonemason then chiseled, or chipped, the rocks into the necessary shapes. The rocks were then put on a wooden sled or on rollers and were hauled out of the quarry by oxen. Men lifted the extremely heavy blocks of marble or other rock into place using a winch. They climbed wooden scaffolding and guided each new rock into place.

Once the blocks were in place, the men used lead staples to connect them. The staples were hidden from view by the next row of blocks. Notice the large pieces of rock used to build this temple to Apollo in Delphi, Greece.

Sailing Ships

The ancient Greeks needed the sea to live. This led them to create new technologies to use the resources of the sea better. The Greeks had several different types of ships. One type was the cargo ship. Sailors used cargo ships to pick up tin, copper, and other goods from nearby places, including Cyprus and Syria. Ships had anchors, which were made of heavy metals, to keep them from drifting off to sea when they were docked in a harbor. The other main type of ship was the trireme, a battleship. This long, wooden ship was built to be fast and light. It was moved through the water by rows of men at oars. Greek fishers crafted nets from rope made of plant and animal fibers. They also used handheld wooden and metal spears to catch and kill fish.

Ancient Greeks built triremes as ▲
warships. Triremes were meant
to sail fast and to smash into the
side of an enemy ship without
being hurt.

Greek fishers used tools made of ▶
stone and metal to catch and
clean fish.

Ancient Greek soldiers crafted and wore heavy armor that protected them from their enemies' weapons.

This statue shows a Greek soldier dressed for battle, holding a spear and a shield.

Weapons

The ancient Greeks made most of their weapons from iron because it was the most available metal. The iron was melted in a furnace or over a fire. When it became soft enough, it was hammered into the shape of the tool that was needed. The weapon used most commonly in ancient Greece was the spear. Only the tip of the spear was made of iron. The handle of the spear was made of wood. In front of their bodies, the soldiers held shields. Shields were made from cured animal hides or hammered metal. Soldiers of ancient Greece were also skilled at using swords, spears called javelins, slingshots, and the bow and arrow against their enemies.

Greeks also used daggers for protection. This one is made of bronze. It has a gold strip in the center and a pattern carved on the blade.

Science and Medicine

When the people of ancient Greece got sick, they prayed to Asclepius, the god of healing, for a cure. Beginning with a man named Hippocrates who lived from about 460 to 377 B.C., the Greeks also had doctors to care for them. Hippocrates believed that people got sick because their bodies were working incorrectly, not because the gods were upset. The study of anatomy was introduced by a Greek man named Herophilus. Another branch of medicine, involving the study of how blood circulates through the body, was introduced by Erasistratus, a Greek man. Although blood circulation was studied in ancient Greece, it was not fully understood for hundreds of years.

Hippocrates (inset) is believed to have taught his pupils under the tree shown here behind the building. Every person who becomes a doctor must take the Hippocratic oath, a promise, based on Hippocrates's ideas about medicine, that the doctor will not harm any patient. ▶

It was a common practice in ancient Greece, and even in the 1700s in America, to bleed patients when they were sick. This meant that a cut was made and some blood was allowed to flow from the person's body.

Tools for Surgery

Although no one knows exactly when the first surgical tools were used, it is believed that Hippocrates performed operations using tools in the 400s B.C. One of the tools he used was the scalpel, which cuts into a sick person's body. Scalpels in ancient Greece were made of steel or bronze. Ancient Greek doctors used dull and sharp hooks during surgery. Doctors used the dull hooks to poke and lift gently small parts, such as blood vessels, inside a person's body. Ancient Greek doctors used sharp hooks for tasks such as holding back the edges of wounds. Ancient Greek doctors did not have medicines to keep their patients from feeling pain, yet they did their best to help sick people get better.

◀ *Amphiarion, a Greek doctor, treats the shoulder of a young man. This relief was carved in the fourth century B.C.*

Astronomy and Mathematics

The ancient Greeks made many important contributions to the modern world. By studying the stars, the Moon, and the Sun, a Greek man named Aristarchus was able to figure out the length of a year. Ancient Greece was home to some of the world's greatest mathematicians, such as Euclid and Pythagoras, too. Many of the ideas of these ancient Greek mathematicians, or people who study math, are still studied today. Euclid wrote a book about geometry that people continue to use, and Ptolemy's *Geography* still serves as the basis for modern atlases, or books filled with maps. It is astounding to think that so many ancient Greek ideas and technologies serve as the basis for the modern world in which we live!

Glossary

anatomy (uh-NA-tuh-mee) The study of the body.

archaeologists (ar-kee-AH-luh-jists) People who study the remains of people or animals to understand how they lived.

architectural (ar-kih-TEK-chuh-rul) Having to do with the style and the creation of buildings.

circulates (ser-kyuh-LAYTS) Moves.

cure (KYUR) To make well.

fertility (fer-TIH-luh-tee) The ability to grow living things.

geography (jee-AH-gruh-fee) The study of Earth's weather, land, countries, people, and businesses.

geometry (jee-AH-meh-tree) A type of math that deals with the measurement of straight lines, circles, and other shapes.

irrigate (EER-ih-gayt) To supply land with water through ditches or pipes.

plumbing (PLUM-ing) Pipes that carry water to and from a building.

resources (REE-sors-ez) Things that occur in nature and that can be used or sold, such as gold, coal, or wool.

rotated (ROH-tayt-ed) Changed a fixed order.

scaffolding (SKA-fold-ing) A stand raised above the ground for workers and materials.

surgical (SER-jih-kul) Having to do with an operation on a hurt or sick person or animal.

technology (tek-NAH-luh-jee) The way that a people do something using tools, and the tools that they use.

winch (WINCH) A machine that has a roller on which a rope is wound for pulling or lifting.

Index

A
anatomy, 18
aqueducts, 9
Aristarchus, 22

B
bathtubs, 9
Bronze Age, 5

C
cisterns, 9
columns, 10
Corinthian style, 10

D
Doric style, 10

G
Geography, 22
geometry, 22
god(s), 13, 18

H
Hippocrates, 18, 21

I
Ionic style, 10
Iron Age, 5

P
plows, 6
Pythagoras, 22

S
scalpel(s), 21
ships, 14
spear(s), 17

T
toilets, 9
trireme, 14

W
weapons, 5, 17
winch, 13

Primary Sources

Cover. Detail of an Attic black-figure pelike decorated with a scene of c shoemaker cutting leather. Eucharides painter. Circa 500–475 B.C. Ashmo Museum. Oxford, United Kingdom. **Inset.** Krater. Gilded bronze. Late fifth ‹ B.C. From a house tomb in Stavroupolis, Greece. Archaeological Museum ‹ Salonica. **Page 4. Left.** Cauldron. Bronze on an iron tripod. Fourth century Found in royal tombs. Vergina, Greece. Archaeological Museum Salonica Greek jewelry. Bronze. Sixth century B.C. From Necropolis of Macchabate Francavilla Maritima, Italy. Museo della Sibaritide Sibari. **Page 7. Inset.** Bl figure kylix showing ritual plowing, possibly a scene from Attic Thesmopho fertility festival. Circa 550 B.C. Athens, Greece. The British Museum. Londc United Kingdom. **Page 8.** Bathroom with ceramic bath. Palace of Nestor. Fourteenth century B.C. Mycenaean. Pylos, Greece. **Page 11. Top left.** Co columns. Temple of Olympian Zeus (Olympieion). Begun in 515 B.C. by P the Younger. Continued in 174 B.C. by Antiochus IV Epiphanes. Finished i 124–125 by Roman Emperor Hadrian. Athens, Greece. **Top Right.** Colur Ionic capital. Delphi, Greece. **Bottom.** Doric columns. Temple of Hera (He Late seventh century B.C. Olympia, Greece. **Page 12.** Polygonal wall. Befc terrace of the Temple of Apollo. Sixth century B.C. Delphi, Greece. **Page 1** Trireme with nine oarsmen. Relief. Marble. Classical Greek. Acropolis Mus Athens, Greece. **Page 16. Left.** Front view of the West Pediment from Tem Aphaia. Circa 490 B.C. Staatliche Antikensammlungen und Glyptothek. **C‹** Dagger. Bronze with gold strip decoration with spiral patterns. Sixteenth ce B.C. Mycenaean. From Tomb 3, Circle 1. Mycenae, Greece. National Archaeological Museum, Athens. **Right.** Armor. Bronze. Mycenaean. From Greece. Archaeological Museum Nauplia Nafplion. **Page 19.** Hippocrate Marble bust. Circa 330–27 B.C. Musée du Louvre. Paris, France. **Page 2(** Amphiarion, the physician, treats the shoulder of a young man. Votive relie Amphiarios. Fourth century B.C. National Archaeological Museum. Athens, **Bottom.** Doctor bleeding a patient. Red-figure aryballos. Fifth century B.C. C vasepainter. Musée du Louvre. Paris, France.

Web Sites

Due to the changing nature of Internet links, PowerKids Press has developed an online list of Web sites related to the subject of this book. This site is updated regularly. Please use this link to access the list:
www.powerkidslinks.com/psaciv/techgre/